Jerry Pallotta's Math = Fun!™

The Addition Book

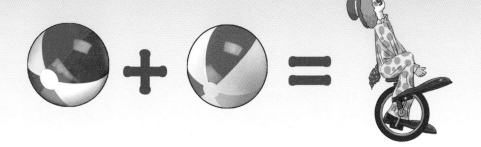

by Jerry Pallotta
Illustrated by Rob Bolster

SCHOLASTIC INC.

New York   Toronto   London   Auckland   Sydney
Mexico City   New Delhi   Hong Kong

Thank you to R. Michael Hechtman and Dr. Judi Hechtman.
— Jerry Pallotta

This book is dedicated to all the people who make their living as clowns.
—Rob Bolster

ISBN 0-439-89637-1

12 11 10 9 8 7 6 5 4 3 2 1   6 7 8 9 10 11/0

Printed in the U.S.A.
First printing, October 2006

CLOWNS PLUS MATH EQUAL FUN!

Here are some math terms that will help you while reading this book.

This is a plus sign. It is used for addition.

 This is a minus sign. It is used for subtraction.

This is an equal sign.
It is used to show that two
or more numbers are equal in value.

 This is a beach ball.
In this book we count and add with colorful beach balls.

This is a clown. There will be no clowning around
on these pages. This is a serious math book.

1 + 1 = 2

Let's start off with a very simple equation. One plus one equals two.
Adding two or more numbers together is called "addition."
This is an addition book.

2+1=3

When the numbers on each side of an equal sign have the same value,
it is called an "equation." Here is another simple equation.
Two plus one equals three.

3+1=4

Three plus one equals what? The answer is four. In math, we say the "sum" is four or the "total" is four. Three plus one equals four.

4+1=5

Four plus one equals five. That is easy to see.
Look closely, though—if we keep on adding one, it is just like counting.
One, two, three, four, five, six, seven, eight, nine, ten.
Counting by one is the same as adding one at a time.

5+1=6

Five plus one equals six. Basic math is called "arithmetic." Arithmetic is addition, subtraction, multiplication, and division. Reading, writing, and arithmetic are very important.

6+1=7

Six plus one equals seven. Uh-oh! Here comes a guy with a pie. Hey, that rhymes. No pie throwing. Splat! Oh, no! You clowns, please stop goofing off while kids are learning basic addition facts.

Okay, you get the idea. Here are all the equations you can
make when you add the number one to each of the numbers one through nine.
In each equation, we can switch the numbers we are adding
and still get the same answer.

1 + 1 = 2   1 + 1 = 2
2 + 1 = 3   1 + 2 = 3
3 + 1 = 4   1 + 3 = 4
4 + 1 = 5   1 + 4 = 5
5 + 1 = 6   1 + 5 = 6
6 + 1 = 7   1 + 6 = 7
7 + 1 = 8   1 + 7 = 8
8 + 1 = 9   1 + 8 = 9
9 + 1 = 10   1 + 9 = 10

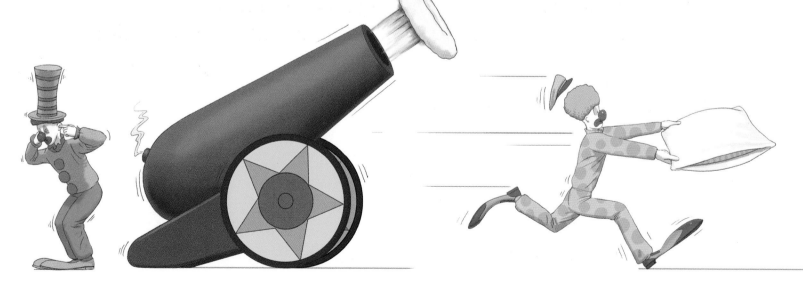

Oops! We forgot a very important equation.

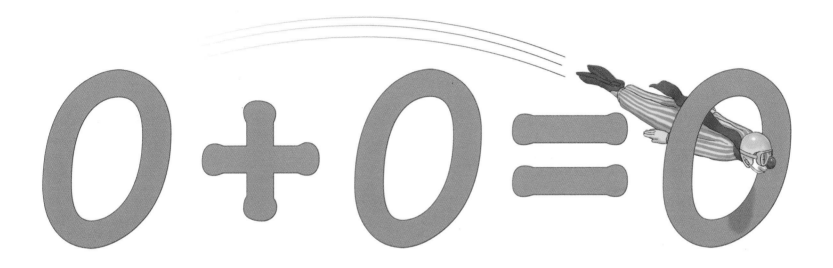

Zero plus zero equals zero.
If you have nothing and then you add nothing to
that, you still have nothing. Zero is a number, but it has no value.

0 + 1 = 1   0 + 6 = 6
0 + 2 = 2   0 + 7 = 7
0 + 3 = 3   0 + 8 = 8
0 + 4 = 4   0 + 9 = 9
0 + 5 = 5   0 +10=10

2 + 2 = 4

Toot! Toot! All aboard!
We are now doing equations that add the same number.
Two plus two equals four. When you add two numbers that are the same,
it is just like doubling the number.

3 + 3 = 6

Three plus three equals six. If you put the answer first, it is called "reversing the equation."   6 = 3 + 3   Six equals three plus three.

4 + 4 = 8

Four plus four is just one of nine addition pairs that add up to eight.
Zero plus eight; one plus seven; two plus six; three plus five; four plus four;
five plus three; six plus two; seven plus one; and eight plus zero.
Do you notice a pattern?

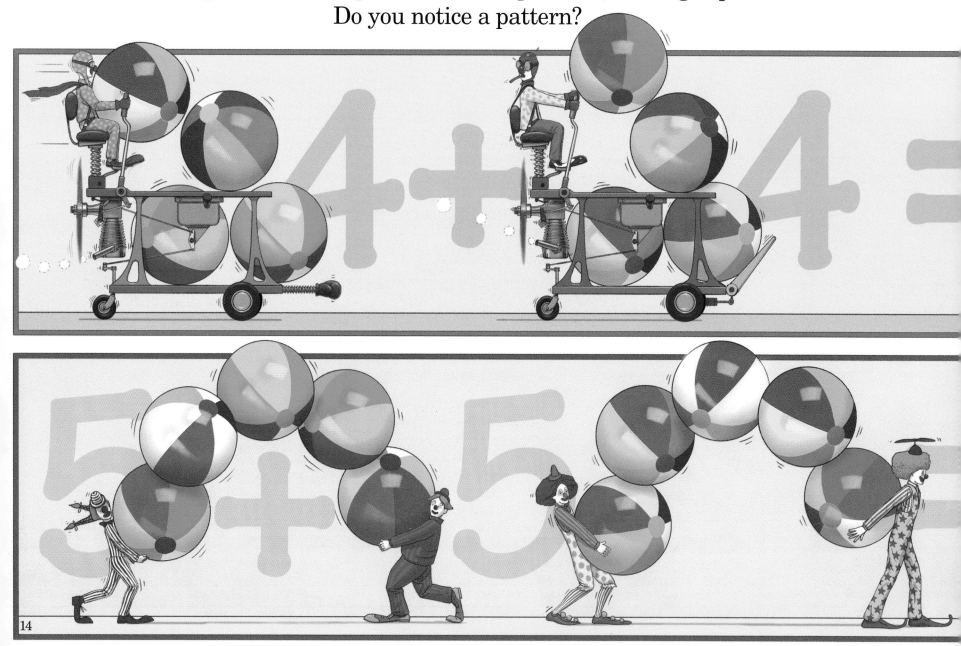

5 + 5 = 10

Five plus five equals ten. Hooray! The clowns made it to ten, a double-digit number! As you can see, the more beach balls we add, the more crowded the pages get. How do you like the arch?

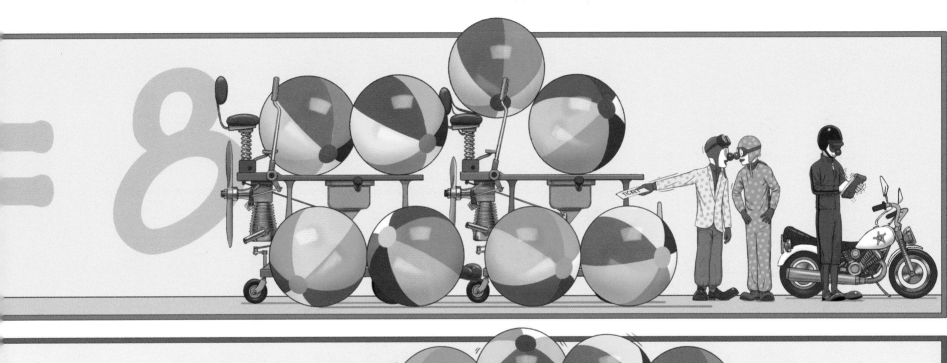

Here are some more addition facts.
Which clown's hairdo is your favorite?

0 + 2 = 2   0 + 3 = 3
1 + 2 = 3   1 + 3 = 4
2 + 2 = 4   2 + 3 = 5
3 + 2 = 5   3 + 3 = 6
4 + 2 = 6   4 + 3 = 7
5 + 2 = 7   5 + 3 = 8
6 + 2 = 8   6 + 3 = 9
7 + 2 = 9   7 + 3 = 10
8 + 2 = 10   8 + 3 = 11
9 + 2 = 11   9 + 3 = 12
10 + 2 = 12   10 + 3 = 13

Each addition fact in this book is made up of "addends" and a "sum." The addends (the numbers you are adding together) are on one side of the equal sign and the sum is on the other.

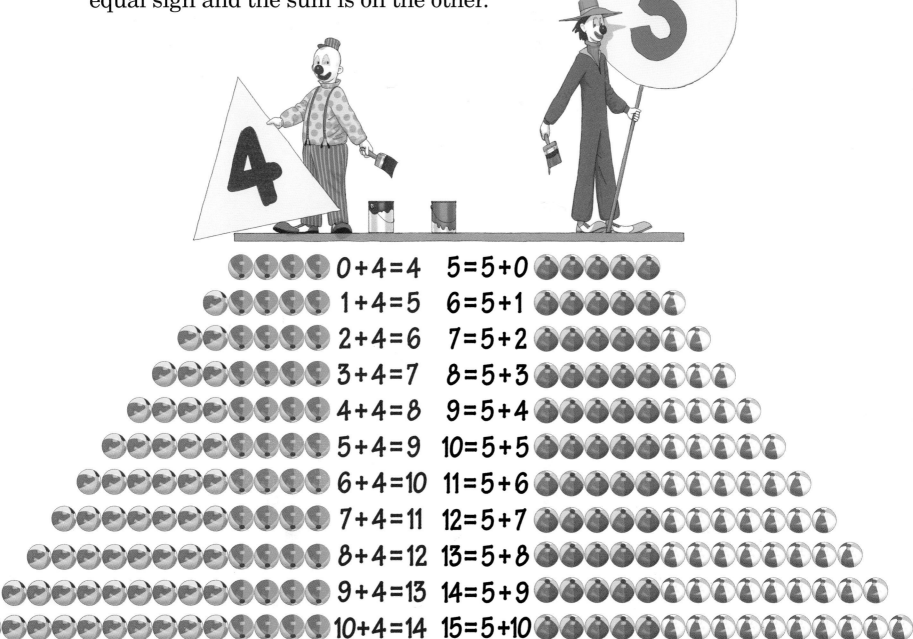

0 + 4 = 4	5 = 5 + 0
1 + 4 = 5	6 = 5 + 1
2 + 4 = 6	7 = 5 + 2
3 + 4 = 7	8 = 5 + 3
4 + 4 = 8	9 = 5 + 4
5 + 4 = 9	10 = 5 + 5
6 + 4 = 10	11 = 5 + 6
7 + 4 = 11	12 = 5 + 7
8 + 4 = 12	13 = 5 + 8
9 + 4 = 13	14 = 5 + 9
10 + 4 = 14	15 = 5 + 10

We used beach balls in this book.
Think of the other balls we could have used.
Oops, we forgot a meatball!

Of course, equations can be done vertically, too. Six plus six equals twelve. Whoa! We have a mistake! There is no need for an equal sign next to the sum when adding numbers vertically. The numbers above the line and the sum below the line are equal in value.

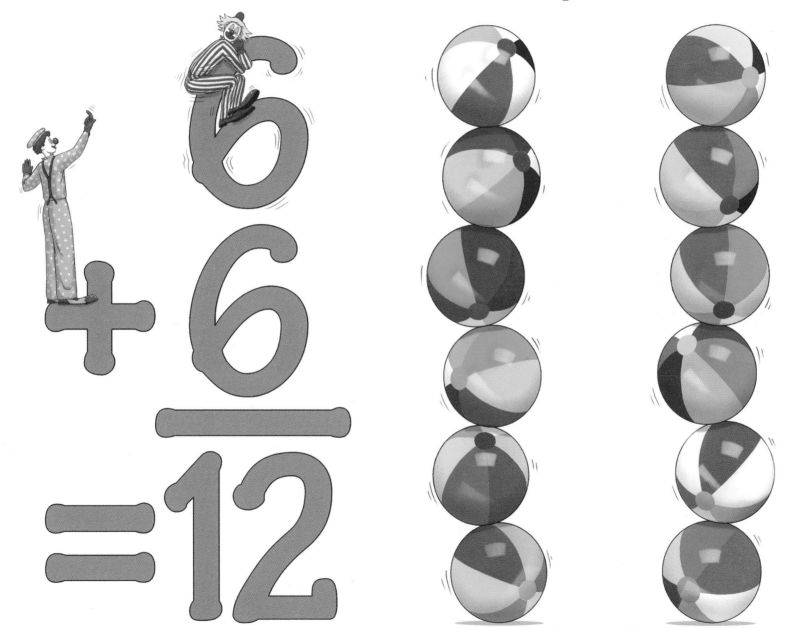

That's better! We have removed the equal sign.
A group of seven plus a group of seven equals fourteen.
Grouping can help you organize, count, and add.

Eight plus eight equals sixteen. Did you know that "math" is an abbreviation for "mathematics," the study of numbers, shapes, and quantities? If your profession were to study math, you would be a mathematician. If you taught math, you would be a math teacher.

It is time to sneak a peek into a classroom.

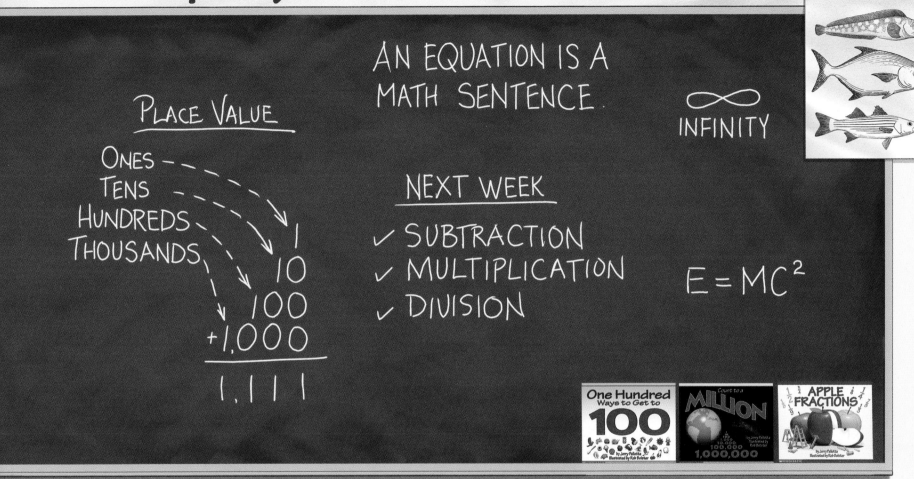

PLACE VALUE

ONES
TENS
HUNDREDS
THOUSANDS

1
10
100
+1,000

1,111

AN EQUATION IS A
MATH SENTENCE.

INFINITY

NEXT WEEK

✓ SUBTRACTION
✓ MULTIPLICATION
✓ DIVISION

$E = MC^2$

One Hundred Ways to Get to 100

Count to a MILLION
1,000
10,000
100,000
1,000,000

APPLE FRACTIONS

Shhh! There is a class in progress. It's math time.
The teacher is showing the students that you can add as many
numbers as you like. There can be big numbers, small numbers,
hard equations, easy equations, lots of numbers, or just a few.

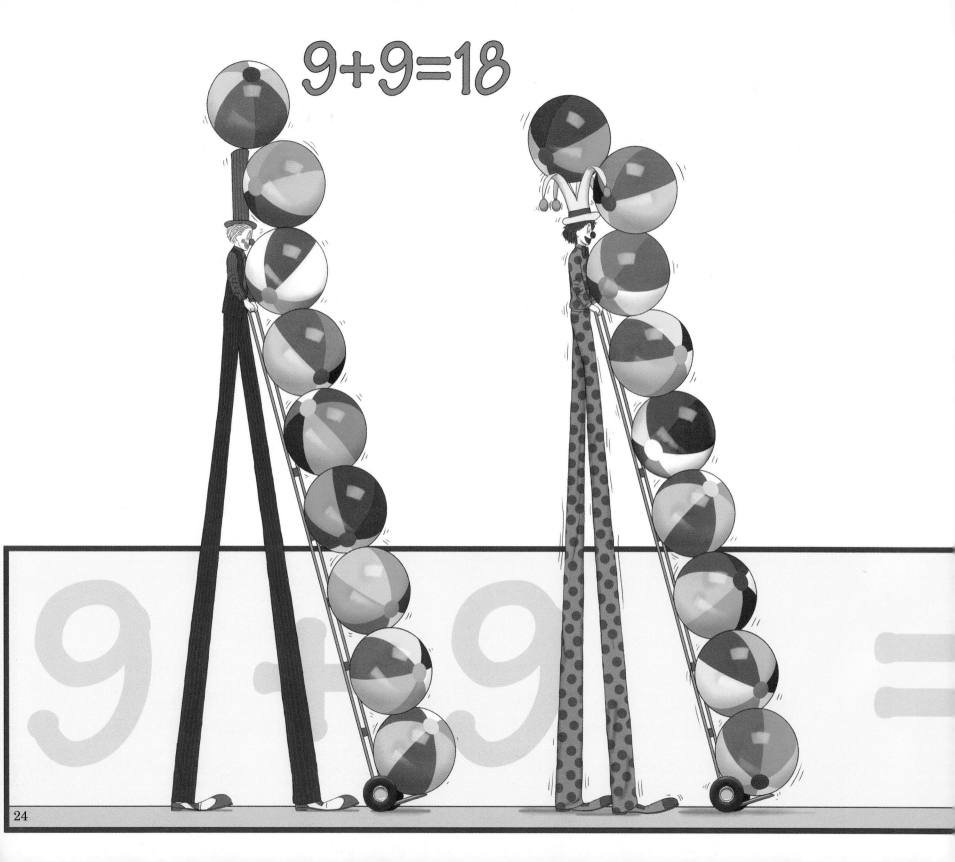

While you are adding nine plus nine, remember this . . .
there is no such thing as the biggest number in the world.
If you add one more number to it, the number becomes larger.

10+10=20

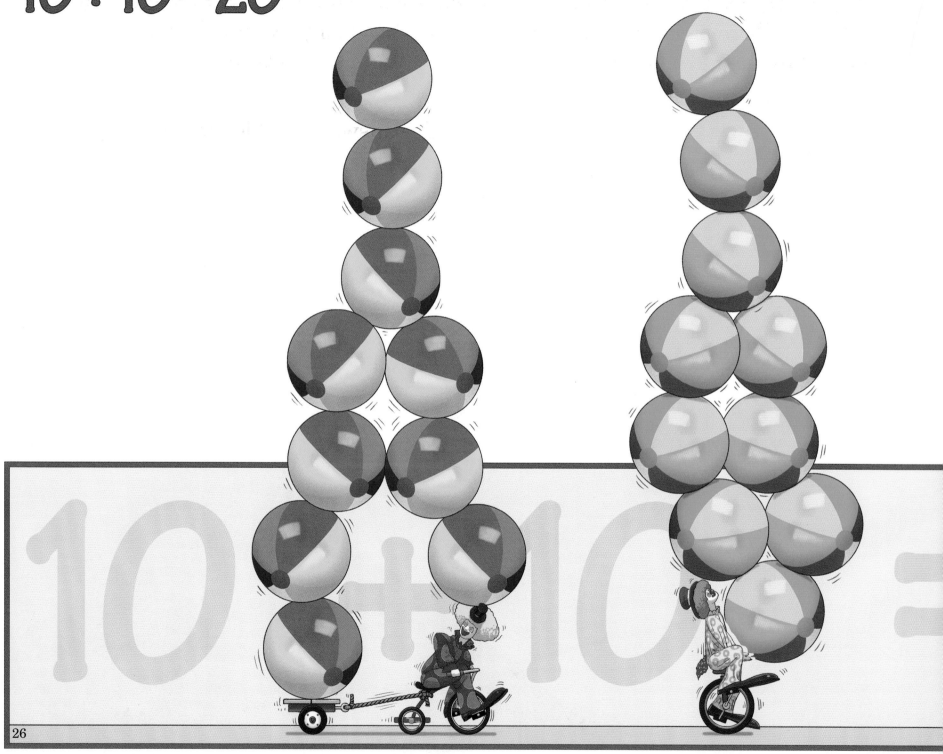

Ten plus ten equals twenty. This is our first equation that adds double-digit numbers. Here is a challenge! Make simple equations by adding only two numbers at a time. How many combinations can you make using the numbers zero through nine?

The answer is hidden on this page.

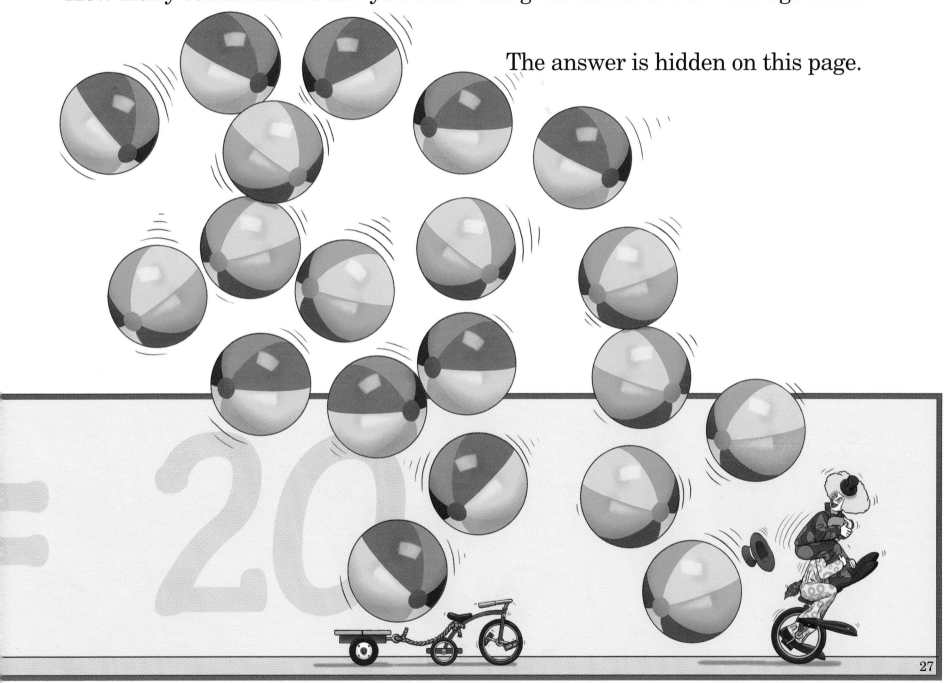

1+1+1=3

Here is a change of pace. Let's add three numbers! One plus one plus one equals three. A math teacher might say we added three "integers" or three "single-digits" or three "addends."

$1 + 2 + 3 = 6$

One plus two plus three equals six. How can you add these numbers?
We already learned that one plus two equals three. We also learned that
three plus three equals six. You do not have to add all the numbers at once.
Two at a time is fine.

25,000,000

Are you afraid of big numbers? How about this number? Twenty-five million!
In the United States and Canada there are about
twenty-five million kids in grades K, 1, 2, 3, 4, and 5.

twenty-five million

Twenty-five million plus one equals twenty-five million and one.
This is what it would look like if all twenty-five million kids
lost their beach balls at the ocean.

We end this addition book with this equation:
Three minus one equals two. If you have three beach balls and somebody removes one of them, you will have two beach balls left over. Hey, that's subtraction!

Subtraction is the opposite of addition.